# 1,000

## CHARACTER

## REACTIONS

*from head to toe*

VALERIE HOWARD

# CONTENTS

# INTRODUCTION

Are your characters always nodding or sighing?

(Did you just nod and sigh?)

If so, this is the book for you! Jam-packed with character reactions and motions that go far beyond the usual nod, sigh, shrug, and frown, everyone should find something in this book that works for their story.

We all know it's important to vary our character's reactions so as not to create boring and trite people no one wants to read about. One easy way to vary reactions is to change the body part your character reacts with.

Though your character *could* always react to new information or an external stimulant with their eyes, it's not recommended to write an entire story that way. Your character's got more than eyes, so they should do more than stare, glare, wink, and blink.

This book is divided up by body part, starting with the head, going down to the toes, then looking internally at what can happen with a character's veins, muscles, and bones when they react to an external stimulant.

This book is not divided up by emotions, but there are some quick emotion tags or suggestions here and there. The reason for this is that a character can bite her lip in rage, irritation, impatience, or in a playfully flirtatious manner. Or he can slouch because of fear, disappointment, shame or fatigue—it's up to you and the context of your story.

I suggest you take a reaction from these lists and put your own spin on it to make it uniquely yours, and uniquely your character's. I've added some lines at the end of each section where you can add your own reactions for each part of the body, too.

Mix and match the reactions to create almost endless possibilities. Your character can yank on her pigtail *and* groan to show her immense frustration. Your character can stick out his tongue *and* cross his eyes to show he doesn't have a care in the world. Beware of stringing too many reactions together in a row, though. Three or more will sound more like a grocery list than a reasonable reaction.

If you're having trouble thinking about what your character would do to react, you can always physically act out the scene and see what your body does and take notes. (Confession: I do this a lot.)

To keep track of which body parts you've

used (or overused) in your story, download the free PDF checklist at my website under the "Resources" tab and make a tally mark next to each body part you write about to see where you are clustering your reactions and where you might need to spread the love.

My website is: www.ForIndieAuthors.com.
Ready to begin? Let's go!

# HEAD

Shaking head once or repeatedly
Nodding head over and over, unable to stop
Giving a curt nod
Tilting head to the side
Tipping head up or down or side to side
Throwing head back in laughter (evil or otherwise)
Banging head on table or other surface
Head feeling suddenly heavy or full of cement
Resting head in hands
Burying head in arms or knees
Ducking head to avoid showing face
Hanging head in shame
Rubbing back of head in confusion or thought
Head feeling like it's spinning
Feeling lightheaded
Feeling suddenly dizzy or tipsy
Head buzzing
Tugging on a hood or cap to hide
Feeling faint
Fainting
Turning head toward a voice or noise
Head feeling like it will float off body
Head pounding with every tick of clock

Rocking head back and forth in disbelief
Rolling head between shoulders to ease tension
Head swimming

_____

_____

_____

_____

_____

_____

_____

_____

_____

_____

_____

_____

# HAIR

Plucking hairs out of head in boredom
Pulling on locks of hair in frustration
Yanking on own braid or ponytail
Raking fingers through hair
Twirling hair around fingers
Brushing hair back behind shoulders
Smoothing hair down if self-conscious
Blowing hair out of face
Combing hair absentmindedly with fingers
Brushing hair with violent strokes
Wrestling frizzy hair into place
Tucking stray hairs behind ear
Attacking knots in hair with brush or comb
Hair standing on end
Doing an uppity hair-flip
Making sure every hair is perfectly in place
Sweeping bangs out of eyes
Hair feeling heavy
Hair feeling on fire
Hair feeling itchy
Gripping/seizing clumps of hair in frustration
Examining/inspecting/plucking white or gray hairs
Tucking hair in hat or hood to hide its color/length

Rolling strand of hair between thumb and pointer
Messing hair up on purpose
Covering facial hair to appear less conspicuous
Chewing on split ends/bottom of braid

_____

_____

_____

_____

_____

_____

_____

_____

_____

_____

_____

# SCALP

Scalp blazing with heat
Scalp itching
Scalp tingling
Scalp crawling as if with lice
Picking at scalp
Scalp feeling tight or shrunken
Ball cap or hat feeling suddenly too small or tight
Hat feeling suddenly too itchy or hot
Digging nails into scalp, trying to stop thoughts
Scratching back of scalp while averting gaze
Cradling scalp in hands to show remorse

_____

_____

_____

_____

_____

# BRAIN

Brain feeling waterlogged
Brain feeling slushy
Brain buzzing with activity
Thoughts swirling through mind
Thoughts or images pinging back and forth
Thoughts becoming cloudy and murky
Imagining horrible outcomes
Vivid images parading across mind
Memories flashing across the mind's eye
Daydreaming
Having dreams that feel real
Having a terrifying nightmare
Experiencing Deja Vu
Racing thoughts
Brain flooding with questions
Arguing internally
Internally chiding self
Launching into an internal pep talk
Having the sensation of falling/sinking in a pit
Having the sensation of floating on a cloud
Synapses all firing at once
Brain shutting down, unable to think
Brain becoming fatigued, thinking crazy thoughts

Brain feeling like it's drying up or shriveling
Brain feeling super smart or big
Brain feeling on fire or smoking from thinking
Forgetting things, losing train of thought
Feeling invisible, ignored, or unimportant
Feeling stupid or disrespected
Getting drunk
Getting high

_____

_____

_____

_____

_____

_____

_____

_____

_____

# FOREHEAD

Forehead wrinkling
Forehead slicking with sweat
Slapping or hitting forehead with palm
Banging forehead against a surface
Wiping moisture off forehead
Pressing fingers against forehead
Tapping forehead with pencil or finger
Forehead baking with a fever
Resting forehead in hand(s)
Splaying back of hand on forehead as if faint
Poking forehead with thumb to jog memory
Banging forehead with fists to stop crazy thoughts

_____

_____

_____

_____

_____

# TEMPLES

Rubbing/massaging temple(s)
Sudden headache
Tapping fingers on temple to think
Holding a gun to temple—real or finger-gun
Putting fingers of one hand to temple and pressing
Temples pounding with each beat of heart
Temples pulsating to drumbeat of loud music
Temples feeling a squeezing, vice-like pressure
Temples feeling like they may burst or explode
Pushing on both temples to stop line of thought
Holding fingers up to temples as if getting a vision

_____

_____

_____

_____

_____

# Eyebrows

Raising eyebrows in interest
Arching one eyebrow in disbelief
Eyebrows furrowing
Eyebrows knitting together
Waggling eyebrows suggestively
Wiggling one eyebrow up and down
Lowering eyebrows
Plucking eyebrows with a vengeance
Giving someone the "hairy eyebrow"
Eyebrows flying to hairline in surprise
Eyebrows drooping with fatigue or depression

---

---

---

---

---

# EYELIDS

Eyelids twitching
Eyelids falling down on own accord
Eyelids hooding over eyes
Eyelids becoming heavy with boredom
Blinking faster
Blinking slower
Blinking several times before speaking
Blinking erratically with crazed expression
Eyelids scrunching closed to block out bad news
Eyelids snapping open in surprise
Squinting
Winking

_____

_____

_____

_____

# EYES

Eyes bulging
Eyes widening
Eyes suddenly popping open during sleep
Eyes burning
Eyes becoming dry or scratchy
Rubbing eyes
Rolling eyes
Eyes watering
Adjusting glasses while fidgeting
Glowering
Scowling
Glaring
Eyes greedily drinking in view with wonder/awe
Eyes turning big and round as saucers
Tear slipping from corner of eye
Eyes sparkling, laughing
Eyes brightening
Squeezing eyes shut in pain
Eyelashes fluttering
Leering at someone
Lowering gaze to feet or ground
Lifting gaze to sky or ceiling
Gaze bouncing back and forth between objects

Gaze stuck on a person or object
Watching or checking a timer or clock constantly
Making eye contact
Avoiding eye contact
Narrowing eyes
Crossing eyes
Staring at someone or something
Looking through someone or something
Refusing to blink
Eyes glazing over
Covering eyes
Stars sparkling in vision
Vision tunneling
Vision clouding, darkening, or fading
Vision brightening to blinding white light
Vision turning blurry
Doing a double-take
Watching out of the corner of eye
Stealthily watching over top of book or newspaper
Giving someone a knowing look
Giving an incredulous look
Sending someone a pointed look
Shooting daggers at someone across the room
Eyes playing tricks
Seeing something that isn't there at second glance
Giving someone a sideways glance
Eyes not adjusting to sudden darkness/light
Pretending not to see someone/something
Giving someone a death stare
Pretending to be asleep to avoid conversation

# NOSE

Nose twitching
Nose scrunching
Turning up nose at something
Nostrils flaring
Picking nose
Pinching bridge of nose
Plugging nose
Putting back of hand to nose to block a scent
Breathing quickly through nose
Breathing heavily through nose
Breathing slowly through nose
Noticing a specific smell
Smelling something that isn't really there
Remembering a nostalgic smell
Tapping end of nose in thought or as in "Bingo!"
Snorting
Holding back a snort
Blowing nose loudly to annoy or draw attention
Twisting/playing with nose ring
Looking down nose at someone
Sneezing
Suppressing a sneeze
Nasal passages narrowing

Nose feeling too big and bulbous
Shoving nose in a book
Shoving nose in someone else's face
Pretending to sniffle
Wiping nose with hankie to cover up a snicker

_____

_____

_____

_____

_____

_____

_____

_____

_____

_____

# CHEEKS

Flushing
Blushing
Cheeks burning hot
Cheeks tingling
Cheeks hurting from smiling too much
Pressing hands to cheeks in embarrassment
Blowing cheeks up, inflating like a balloon
Cheeks twitching in embarrassment
Pushing tongue into cheek
Sucking in cheeks while thinking
Pinching cheeks to wake up
Nibbling on inside of cheeks
Bringing object to cheek to nuzzle it
Pressing cheek against someone's chest
Stroking cheek in deep thought
Cheeks tightening with disapproval
Slapping cheeks to snap out of panic
Lightly touching cheek where a kiss had been
Holding a cheek as if slapped with harsh words

# EARS

Ears ringing
Ears burning
Ears freezing
Ears perking up
Tugging on earlobe
Hearing everything as if under water
Suddenly unable to hear because thoughts are loud
Ignoring someone on purpose
Ears stopped up with silence
Covering ears with hands
Putting fingers inside of ears
Scratching at ears when hearing something awful
Ears straining to listen to something quiet/far away
Drawing an air-circle around ear to say "crazy"
Twisting/fiddling with earring
Ripping earring out of ear
Pressing ear to door/wall to listen more closely
Words echoing in ears
Hurtful words stinging ears
Shouting booming through ears
Eardrum shattering
Ears picking up an out-of-place sound

# LIPS

Upper lip sweating
Lower lip trembling
Licking lips
Biting or chewing lip(s)
Lips turning up into a smile
Sucking lip(s) inside mouth
Frowning
Sneering
Smile slipping
Forcing a smile
Faking a smile
Lips pressed in a straight line
Snarling
Whistling
Kissing a person or object
Puckering lips with a sour taste
Stroking mustache
Twisting handlebar mustache
Wiping food off of mustache
Worrying lips
Catcalling
Smacking lips to annoy someone
Blowing raspberries with lips

Drawing lipstick on lips slowly and deliberately
Sticking out lower lip in giant pout

_____

_____

_____

_____

_____

_____

_____

_____

_____

_____

_____

# MOUTH

Side of mouth quirking upward
Mouth gaping open
Mouth watering
Mouth drying
Making popping noises with mouth
Blowing a kiss
Making a kissy face
Making a fishy face
Covering mouth in shock
Yawning
Drooling
Spitting on ground or at someone
Opening mouth to speak, then snapping it shut
Foaming at the mouth
Keeping mouth shut with effort
Doing a spit-take
Swishing drink around in mouth to buy time
Snapping mouth shut to keep in a laugh or gasp
Pouting
Food turning to dust in mouth
Mouth becoming sticky
Popping gum
Smacking gum loudly to annoy or gain attention

Giving a lopsided grin
Slowly sipping a drink while in deep thought
Relishing the taste of a kiss
Letting out a belch to appear sloppy/indifferent

---

---

---

---

---

---

---

---

---

---

---

---

# TONGUE

Clicking tongue
Sticking out tongue
Blowing raspberries with tongue
Tongue suddenly heavy
Tongue sticking to roof of mouth
Running tongue along teeth or gums
Licking lips
Biting down on tongue to keep quiet
Having bitter taste on tongue/in mouth
Almost tasting a familiar food without eating it
Having a sudden sour taste on tongue/in mouth
Tongue seizing up, unable to form words
Chewing on tongue
Twisting tongue ring around inside mouth
Tongue feeling free and loose, speaking too much
Suddenly becoming thirsty or parched
Twisting gum around tongue in boredom
Tongue going rogue, telling a secret without trying

# TEETH

Teeth chattering
Teeth grinding
Teeth gnashing
Chewing on inside of cheek
Biting down hard on an object
Biting someone
Biting self
Biting or chomping the air in anguish
Sucking air through teeth in pain
Baring teeth
Tearing a package open with teeth in frustration
Whistling through teeth
Wiggling a loose tooth with tongue or finger
Nibbling on pencil/pen
Picking food out of braces
Taking forever to brush teeth to avoid or annoy
Clicking teeth together loudly or repeatedly
Snarling at someone or something
Opening a beer bottle with teeth to appear tough
Yanking out an aching tooth
Flossing incessantly or obsessively
Checking teeth for bits of food
Mouth feeling dirty after regretful kiss

Using mouthwash after lying/flirting/flattering

_____

_____

_____

_____

_____

_____

_____

_____

_____

_____

_____

_____

_____

# JAW

Jaw locking shut
Jaw hanging open
Jaw clenching
Jaw tightening
Working jaw back and forth
Jaw dropping and snapping shut again
Popping jaw repeatedly
Setting jaw with determination
Squaring jaw
Jaw feeling as if it might break with teeth clenched
Jaw trembling with rage
Jaw feeling like a spring wound with tension

_____

_____

_____

_____

_____

# CHIN

Chin quivering
Chin tipping up in a snobby manner
Tucking chin low in shame
Rubbing chin
Stroking beard or stubble
Tapping chin in thought
Throwing chin up in defiance
Resting chin on base of palm
Resting chin on knees
Propping chin on both hands innocently
Chin dropping to the floor in shock
Dribbling water on chin in hurry to speak
Scratching chin in deep thought
Chin feeling pinned to chest

# FACE

Making a sour face
Making a goofy face
Face crumpling
Sporting a smug expression
Countenance falling
Hiding/shielding face with hands, hair, or object
Beaming
Face glowing
Countenance brightening
Face darkening
Face turning purple with rage
Face draining of color
Face turning green with illness
Giving a dumbfounded expression
Twisting face in disgust
Cringing
Shoving face in someone else's face
Maintaining a blank expression
Grimacing
Schooling an inappropriate expression
Wiping a smile off face
Face falling to dirt in worship
Stuffing face with chocolate or other candy

Smothering face with pillow
Flopping face-first onto bed or sofa

_____

_____

_____

_____

_____

_____

_____

_____

_____

_____

_____

_____

_____

# NECK

Neck craning
Neck cracking
Neck bending away from someone
Neck bowing
Massaging back of neck
Rolling neck back and forth
Hand flying to front of neck
Vein in neck bulging
Neck turning red or getting hot
Blush creeping up neck
Pressing a knife into neck
Folding hands and resting them at back of neck
Scratching neck in thought
Clawing at neck if breathing is difficult
Dragging fingernails down neck in pain/anguish
Turning neck as far as it can go to watch someone
Itchy sensation traveling up or down neck
Elongating neck
Neck feeling tight or stiff
Feeling as if a heavy chain is strangling neck
Unbuttoning top button of shirt to cool down
Loosening a tie
Adam's apple bobbing with nerves

Scarf suddenly feeling like it's strangling
Noticing weight of a necklace or locket
Neck feeling weak, as if can't hold head up

_____

_____

_____

_____

_____

_____

_____

_____

_____

_____

_____

_____

# THROAT

Swallowing around a lump in throat
Swallowing loudly
Choking on a swallow
Coughing on spit
Gulping
Gagging
Throat closing up
Choking on food or drink (or rage)
Gasping
Throat burning
Throat feeling suddenly dry
Throat swelling
Throat thickening with emotion
Clearing throat to draw attention or buy time
Acid filling throat
Bile rising into throat
Clutching at throat in panic
Squeezing throat to choke self
Throat feeling raw
Throat narrowing as thin as a straw
Throat getting raspy
Throat suddenly expanding to let in air
Giggle bubbling up in throat

Making a strangled noise with throat
Esophagus letting out a strange noise
Choking down disgusting food to please someone

# VOICE

Muttering under breath
Letting out a yip
Whooping
Growling
Singing
Grunting
Crying
Sobbing
Wailing
Squeaking
Squealing
Groaning
Moaning
Humming
Babbling
Whimpering
Blubbering
Grumbling
Stuttering
Laughing
Giggling
Twittering
Fussing

Sulking
Flirting
Speaking gibberish
Shouting an expletive
Whispering harshly
Hurling insults
Crying out to God
Whispering a quick prayer
Screaming in fright
Screaming in delight
Suddenly losing voice in surprise
Being unable to summon words due to shock
Eating or drinking something to avoid speaking
Using clipped words when irritated
Keeping absolutely silent
Shrieking until hoarse
Interrupting someone
Readily agreeing with someone to avoid conflict
Using a lot of big, fancy words to appear smart
Interrupting oneself and starting over repeatedly
Launching into a long speech or rant
Voice trailing off into nothingness
Suddenly halting in mid-sentence
Howling in pain or like a wolf
Asking incessant questions
Talking in a baby voice
Regressing to an old accent or way of talking
Accidental laugh escaping too loudly
Voice turning melodic
Talking in a sing-song, teasing tone
Rattling off a long list of facts

Speaking in a robotic, rehearsed tone
Lashing out with cruel, hateful words
Screaming into a pillow
Switching to sarcastic tone
Using harsh tone
Lying to cover up guilt
Denying knowledge or involvement
Threatening someone
Shouting out an accidental "Yes!" or "No!"
Starting a false rumor about someone to misdirect
Apologizing profusely
Accusing someone of false or horrible things
Becoming argumentative
Becoming petty
Singing someone's praises
Complaining about weather or schedule
Starting to name off someone's flaws or misdeeds
Starting to read out loud to drown out talking
Calling out "Halt!" or "Stop!"
Changing topic of conversation abruptly
Softening tone

_____

_____

_____

_____

# Shoulders

Shoulders going rigid
Shoulders sagging
Shoulders drooping
Throwing shoulders back in attention
Shrugging
Cracking or popping shoulders
Rolling shoulders forward
Rolling shoulders backward
Rotating shoulders to loosen up
Shoulders shaking with silent laughter
Lifting shoulders to earlobes
Coat feeling suddenly too heavy or hot
Shoulders feeling laden with a burden
Shoulders feeling as if a sudden burden has lifted
Rolling a bare shoulder suggestively
Standing shoulder-to-shoulder to show equality

---

---

---

# TORSO

Fidgeting
Squirming
Shifting weight of body forward or backward
Shivering with sudden cold
Tightening or going rigid with fear
Shaking with anger
Trembling uncontrollably
Quivering with anticipation
Lunging at someone
Rushing toward someone in rage
Hips swaying to music—real or imaginary
Doubling over in pain or with anxiety
Shrinking away from someone or something
Startling in surprise
Curling body around an object to protect it
Leaning away from unwanted object, person, place
Leaning heavily against an object to stay upright
Leaning lazily on wall to appear casual/indifferent
Curling up in a corner
Hiding under a blanket or bed
Towering over someone
Cowering under someone
Twisting around to limber up/loosen up

Writhing in anguish
Wrestling someone to the ground
Tackling someone
Ripping off clothing

_____

_____

_____

_____

_____

_____

_____

_____

_____

_____

_____

_____

# CHEST

Tightening sensation in chest
Chest swelling with hope
Chest puffing out with pride
Chest deflating with defeat
Chest feeling suddenly painful
Clutching at chest over heart
Rubbing sternum
Folding arms across chest
Heart pounding through chest
Pressing palm into chest to try to suppress sorrow
Chest bumping someone to celebrate
Unbuttoning/buttoning shirt buttons
Fiddling with jacket zipper—zipping, unzipping
Chest feeling tight or like it's imploding
Chest feeling like it might explode with emotion
Chest feeling burdened and heavy
Chest feeling like it's being crushed in a vice
Crossing arms across chest in protective stance

# HEART

Heart thumping wildly
Heartbeat doubling or tripling in speed
Heart skipping a beat
Heart stopping
Heart pausing for a beat
Heart hiccuping
Heart pounding out an erratic rhythm
Heart aching with grief
Valves of heart feeling clogged or sluggish
Pain shooting through heart
Ice stabbing through heart
Shock of fear or panic zipping through heart
Heart feeling as if it will explode or catch fire
Heart suddenly feeling homesick
Heart feeling clogged with guilt
Heart feeling heavy with sorrow
Heart feeling as if it's shredded to tiny pieces
Warmth spreading up arm and into heart
Heart sinking in disappointment
Feeling as if drumsticks are banging on heart

# LUNGS

Lungs burning
Lungs collapsing
Lungs cinching tighter, not letting air in
Lungs expanding with a deep intake of air
Lungs feeling as if shriveling or shrinking
Lungs feeling as if they are filling with water
Lungs feeling as if they aren't working
Lungs going into a spasm
Lungs hardening like concrete
Lungs rattling or wheezing
Effervescent feeling in lungs
Lungs feeling unable to exhale
Lungs emptying on their own without permission
Sighing
Blowing breath out in slow stream
Hyperventilating
Inhaling sharply
Holding breath in anticipation or to avoid detection
Breath catching in surprise
Gasping for air
Taking a long drag of cigarette or cigar
Suddenly feeling like the air is poisonous
Feeling out of breath

Feeling like can't catch breath for a long time
Feeling like can't take a deep enough breath
Needing to breathe some fresh air
Feeling like the air is too thick to breathe
Coughing to cover up what someone else is saying
Faking a cough
Sucking air greedily after holding breath
Feeling like clean air is cleansing from inside out
Refusing to breathe in toxins
Forcing self to slow breathing down
Forcing self to take a deep breath and relax
Starting square breathing or Lamaze breathing
Asthma symptoms starting
Having an asthma attack in response to bad news
Breathing loudly on purpose to annoy

_____

_____

_____

_____

_____

_____

_____

# STOMACH

Stomach churning
Stomach roiling
Stomach aching
Feeling nauseous
Vomiting
Patting/rubbing stomach as if satisfied with meal
Holding stomach because of sudden shock
Grabbing stomach in pain
Stomach growling or gurgling
Stomach lurching
Stomach tightening
Stomach growing hard
Stomach feeling overly full
Stomach feeling hollow
Butterflies in stomach
Stomach somersaulting
Stomach doing a flip
Sucking stomach in to appear thinner
Suddenly craving a familiar/particular food
Suddenly losing appetite
Feeling bloated
Stomach contents boiling
Stomach contents turning into bricks or rocks

Giving a deep belly laugh
Expanding stomach with air to relax
Stomach filling with gas/becoming gassy

_____

_____

_____

_____

_____

_____

_____

_____

_____

_____

_____

_____

# BACK

Straightening back
Slouching
Hunching in shame
Elongating spine
Pressing back against the wall to disappear
Shiver traveling up or down spine
Leaning forward
Bending backwards as far as body will allow
Twisting around to look behind
Bowing down to someone
Arching back
Cinching shoulder blades together
Feeling someone's eyes staring at back
Stretching spine unnaturally to appear taller
Cracking/popping back to relieve pressure
Doing a back flip

_____

_____

_____

# BOTTOM

Scooting forward in a chair
Sitting on the edge of bench
Falling into a sitting position
Leaning back into a chair or couch
Sitting perfectly still
Shifting weight in seat
Clenching buttocks tightly to prepare for beating
Pulling at hem of skirt to provide better coverage
Self-consciously blocking rear with book or hands
Finding a comfortable way to sit on awkward chair
Sticking rear end out for attention

_____

_____

_____

_____

_____

# ARMS

Arms feeling heavy
Arms becoming dead weight
Arms going numb
Arms aching to hold something or someone
Arms opening wide for an embrace
Crossing arms in a huff
Flailing arms in panic
Waving arms madly in rage
Wrapping arms around body in loose hug
Shielding pregnant belly with arms
Throwing something into a wall to break
Chucking something as far away as possible
Grabbing and carrying a large armload in a huff
Shoving large pieces of furniture out of the way
Shifting a car into drive or park with force
Slamming door on someone
Armpits suddenly getting sticky
Armpits suddenly getting slick
Sniffing own armpits
Suddenly becoming aware of own body odor
Resting elbows on knees in exhaustion
Raising a trophy or prize above head in victory
Flapping arms, imitating a chicken, to egg on

Holding arms out beside body to bask in glory/sun
Elbowing way through a crowd
Using elbow as a weapon
Linking arms with a friend or to feign friendship
Brandishing a weapon

_____

_____

_____

_____

_____

_____

_____

_____

_____

_____

_____

# HANDS

Pumping fist in victory
Wringing hands
Fanning face for some air
Clapping with glee
Quickly hiding something in closed fist
Waving away a statement
Waving frantically to say hello
Waving both hands to get attention or help
Putting hands up to block a blow or statement
Hitting a door frame or window sill
Slapping face to wake up or snap out of panic
Slapping someone's cheek if offended
Punching a fist through a wall or window
Throwing punches at an enemy
Clenching fist until it hurts
Flexing hand over and over
Crushing an object in fist
Ripping or tearing paper/document to shreds
Beating hands on a wall or door
Knocking repeatedly on a door
Banging madly on a door in panic or anger
Pressing palms together firmly
Slamming palms into table

Holding hands out with palms up
Flinging hands above head in celebration
Reaching for someone only to pull away
Grabbing someone, handling them roughly
Playfully punching someone in jest
Rubbing hands together greedily
Snapping a pencil or twig in half
Propping hands on hips
Giving someone the middle finger
Flashing the "OK" sign
Forming the "I love you" sign
Stuffing hands deep into pockets
Throwing down napkin/towel to indicate giving up
Resting blade of knife on wrist
Giving someone a high-five
Giving self a high-five if left hanging
Punching/kneading dough violently
Baking a familiar/comforting meal
Keeping hands busy by cleaning/typing/knitting
Banging on piano/keyboard keys
Shaking someone's hand firmly with confidence
Giving a weak handshake
Crushing someone's hand with a handshake
Digging/scrounging around in purse to look busy
Hacking/chopping veggies or food to a pulp
Playing piano music to match mood
Shooting hoops/playing a sport to blow off steam
Steering car erratically to scare someone
Resting hand on back of someone else's to comfort
Resting hand on someone's shoulder
Patting someone on the back

Taking someone's hands to keep them from leaving
Placing one hand on hip with an attitude

_____

_____

_____

_____

_____

_____

_____

_____

_____

_____

_____

_____

_____

# FINGERS

Cracking knuckles
Twiddling thumbs
Awkwardly picking at a spot on clothes
Pinching oneself to make sure not dreaming
Nibbling fingernails
Sucking thumb or another finger
Tapping fingernails on surface
Drumming a beat on a table with pointers
Scratching at a sudden itch
Intertwining fingers and squeezing
Rolling a pencil or round object between fingers
Pushing pointer to lips to shush someone
Fiddling with an object for distraction or comfort
Tugging at clothes, cuffs, or collars
Making clicking noises with fingernails
Shaking finger at someone
Using fingers as a gun
Using pointer as a magic wand
Fumbling and dropping keys in panic or in a hurry
Steepling fingers
Jabbing pointer into someone's chest
Twirling a cigarette
Twisting a wedding/engagement ring around finger

Pressing down hard with pencil and breaking lead
Hooking thumbs around belt loops
Fingers aching to touch something or someone
Fingers itching to play an instrument
Pressing fingers together as if praying or begging
Pressing fingers deep into eye sockets
Giving a thumbs up
Snapping fingers impatiently at wait staff
Snapping fingers in an "I got it" motion
Hooking fingers in suspenders or overall straps
Snapping an elastic waistband over and over
Cleaning dirt out from underneath fingernails
Studying dirt underneath fingernails
Playing with a hangnail
Ripping out a hangnail
Flipping through a scrapbook
Trailing fingers along old photograph
Jabbing buttons on phone
Pressing fingertips to a window with longing
Doodling/scribbling to appear occupied
Stroking pet's fur to ease stress
Writing out a to-do list
Tickling someone

---

---

---

# LEGS

Pacing
Jogging or running to blow off steam or clear head
Crossing legs slowly
Uncrossing legs quickly
Jumping or leaping with joy
Bouncing knees up and down
Knocking knees together
Knees suddenly going weak
Legs turning to jelly or liquid
Doing a happy dance
Widening stance, bracing body for impact
Bringing legs together in attention
Jumping and clicking heels together
Tripping or stumbling after loss of focus
Collapsing to knees in desperation
Kicking something or someone
Stretching out legs to limber up
Quickening pace
Slowing pace
Sashaying away from someone
March over to someone to demand an explanation
Pressing thighs together
Digging nails into thighs

Drumming out a beat on lap
Slapping a knee with a guffaw
Tapping fingers on thigh
Trailing hand along seam of jeans/skirt
Dropping to one knee to propose or beg
Falling to knees in reverence
Scraping/shoving chair backwards quickly
Having the urge to run, but feeling stuck
Kicking dirt, stirring up a cloud of dust
Slowly backing away from someone or something
Slowly approaching someone or something
Creeping up on someone to surprise them
Skipping with happiness
Hopping with excitement
Jumping into a body of water
Jumping off a bridge or cliff
Running to phone to make a call/answer the ring
Limping/hobbling to escape
Faking a limp for sympathy or attention
Feeling like rug is being pulled out from under feet
Legs going wobbly

_____

_____

_____

_____

# FEET

Tapping foot with impatience
Snapping heels together
Propping feet up on surface
Stomping foot in irritation or anger
Turning ankle in tiny, slow circles
Bouncing on balls of feet
Slamming on a gas pedal
Stomping on break pedal—real or imaginary
Wiping feet with sharp motions
Shuffling feet on carpet
Shoes suddenly feeling too tight or uncomfortable
Feet turning to lead, becoming too heavy
Feet sticking, becoming glued to the floor
Tapping foot to beat of music
Feet dancing while seated
Playing footsie with someone under a table
Kicking through wall or window
Swinging feet back and forth while sitting
Ripping shoes/socks off in a hurry
Pulling shoes/socks on in a rush
Stomping around a room
Feet feeling clumsy and bumbling
Dropping everything to run to someone's aid

Falling in step beside someone
Racing someone
Flinging off shoes to walk barefoot in sand/grass
Rocking back and forth on heels

_____

_____

_____

_____

_____

_____

_____

_____

_____

_____

_____

_____

# TOES

Wiggling toes
Curling toes tightly
Toes tingling
Toes feeling numb
Overturning a stone or pebble with toe
Standing on tiptoes to appear taller
Touching something dirty with toe instead of hand
Burying toes in sand to hide them or warm them
Spreading toes wide to relieve internal pressure
Grinding big toe into ground
Grinding a cigarette into ground with toe of shoe
Shifting to point toes toward/away from someone
Quickly hiding/tucking toes under feet
Blood draining to tips of toes

_____

_____

_____

_____

# Skin

Skin prickling with goosebumps
Skin crawling as if with insects
Skin having a sudden flush/redness
Skin dropping in temperature, feeling cold
Skin turning clammy
Breaking out in a hot or cold sweat
Digging at a scab
Picking at a wound
Scratching itches
Skin feeling tight or uncomfortable
Skin feeling darker or lighter in contrast to crowd
Hairs standing upright on skin
Rubbing skin vigorously to warm it
Becoming hypersensitive to touch
Breaking out in hives
Clothes suddenly feeling itchy or uncomfortable
Tearing at skin as if to escape from own body
Covering skin to hide color or imperfection
Skin feeling numb or tingly
Skin feeling dried up and cracked
Feeling a phantom pain of an old injury
Pulling or tugging at skin with nervousness
Pinching rolls of fatty skin in disgust

Trailing fingers over bare skin suggestively
Feeling of electricity passing over skin
Adjusting clothes to show more skin
Adjusting clothes to hide skin

 

_____

_____

_____

_____

_____

_____

_____

_____

_____

_____

_____

_____

# VEINS

Blood boiling
Blood turning to ice
Pulse quickening
Pulse slowing
Pulse pounding or drumming
Increasing blood pressure
Decreasing blood pressure
Veins throbbing
Adrenaline surging through veins
Icy fear shooting through veins
Angry lightning sizzling through veins
Blood rushing through veins at an enormous pace
Blood thickening and turning to slush
Veins narrowing and cutting off blood supply
Blood pooling or rushing to one area of body
Blood draining from one area of body
Veins feeling like they are bulging, about to burst
Veins feeling useless, like blood stopped pumping

# MUSCLES

Going limp
Going rigid
Flexing in anticipation
Lifting weights to blow off steam or to impress
Not moving a muscle in shock
Freezing in place like a statue to hide
Muscles suddenly feeling weak or watery
Muscles coiling, getting ready to spring
Muscles becoming twitchy
Muscles becoming jumpy
Muscles moving as if on auto-pilot
Muscles trembling with overuse
Muscles quivering with tension
Muscles feeling as if they are coming unraveled
Absentmindedly repeating a motion over and over
Muscles feeling fatigued and unable to lift body
Restlessness settling in
Muscles feeling large, strong, and protective

# Bones

Bones suddenly feeling tired
Bones aching with longing
Feeling something is true down to the bones
Bones liquefying
Popping or cracking bones or joints
Bones feeling suddenly old, brittle, or fragile
Bones feeling like molten lava
Bones feeling ice cold

_____

_____

_____

_____

_____

_____

_____

# OTHER ORGANS

Intestines gurgling
Intestines twisting up in painful knots
Bladder almost bursting
Bladder leaking when laughing
Bladder emptying with sudden scare
Bladder drying up
Internal organs rebelling
Liver turning to liquid
Insides hardening into stone
Organs feeling like they are shifting out of place
Insides feeling like they are burning up with illness

_____

_____

_____

_____

_____

# PHONE

*Okay, I know a cell phone isn't exactly part of the body, but some people are so attached to their devices that they might as well be an extra body part. So here are a few reactions a character can play out with their cell.*

Taking a selfie to mark an important moment
Burying face in phone screen
Talking on the phone loudly to be heard by all
Snapping a picture at an inappropriate time
Recording someone making a scene
Checking every ping and notification alert
Ignoring a call
Ignoring a text
Hanging up on someone mid-sentence
Pretending there's bad reception to drop the call
Obsessively texting someone
Patting pocket to make sure phone is there
Shutting down phone to become unreachable
Scrolling through phone to ignore outside world
Pretending to talk on the phone or text to avoid

# ABOUT

VALERIE HOWARD has been a self-published author since 2011. She's a follower of Jesus, the wife of a pastor, the mother and teacher of two energetic boys, a graduate of Bible college, and the author of several novels, plays, non-fiction books, and children's books.

If you liked this book, you may also like:

**1,000 Strong Verbs for Fiction Writers**
**1,000 Helpful Adjectives for Fiction Writers**

(Both free with Kindle Unlimited.)

Get a FREE book at ForIndieAuthors.com

www.Facebook.com/forindieauthors

www.Instagram.com/forindieauthors